THE DRUMMER'S PLAYBOOK

THE ULTIMATE GUIDE FOR THE SERIOUS DRUMMER

by Joe Corsello

 iUniverse®

THE DRUMMER'S PLAYBOOK
THE ULTIMATE GUIDE FOR THE SERIOUS DRUMMER

iUniverse books may be ordered through booksellers or by contacting:

iUniverse
1663 Liberty Drive
Bloomington, IN 47403
www.iuniverse.com
1-800-Authors (1-800-288-4677)

ISBN: 978-1-4917-9986-4 (sc)
ISBN: 978-1-4917-9987-1 (e)

Library of Congress Control Number: 2016915966

Print information available on the last page.

iUniverse rev. date: 12/02/2016

"Dedicated to John Beck of the Eastman School of Music, whose patience enabled me to write this method".

Foreword

Music is an important part of our lives. It brings joy and many other feelings. As a music performer, you want to be able to feel that and bring that to the music. As a music student, you should have some fun right away, but there is going to be some work involved in order to get better. There may be some frustrating moments along the way. Good! That means you are working towards something. No matter what level you are at, as a beginner or experienced professional, you can always get better, and should strive for that. We are always students. And of course, we should strive to make beautiful music.

Joe Corsello has a lot of experience playing with great musicians and also a lot of teaching experience, so he knows about the basic things that need to be mastered in order to play music well. This book clearly demonstrates those things and should help you find some joy in the music

- William Stewart

A special thanks to Ron Nyman, without whose help and guidance this book would not be possible

TABLE OF CONTENTS

THE BASICS FOR DRUM MUSIC

The Music Staff has 5 lines and 4 spaces.

The clef signs most used are the treble clef (sometimes called the G clef), indicated by the sign 𝄞, and the bass clef (sometimes called the F clef), indicated by the sign 𝄢, placed at the beginning of the staff, as:

and

The bass clef is usually used on the drum staff, although some composers use a *"neutral"* clef which appears as:

The drummer will encounter the treble clef only when playing the keyboard percussion instruments, as;

Vibes or Marimba

(music staff)

TIME SIGNATURES

The top number gives the number of counts (beats) per measure. The bottom number gives the value of the note that gets one count (beat).

Example:

3/4 means that there are three counts (beats) per measure and a quarter note gets one count (beat).

4/4 means that there are four counts (beats) per measure and a quarter note gets one count (beat).

NOTES AND THEIR VALUES (in basic quadruple meter)

The **WHOLE** note gets four (4) COUNTS (beats)

The **EIGHTH** note gets a half (½) COUNT (beat)

(bass clef half note)

The **HALF** note gets two (2) COUNTS (beats)

The **SIXTEENTH** note gets a quarter (¼) COUNT (beat)

The **QUARTER** note gets one (1) COUNT (beat)

1

RESTS AND THEIR VALUES (in basic quadruple meter)

The **WHOLE** rest gets four (4) COUNTS (beats)

The **EIGHTH** rest gets a half (½) COUNT (beat)

The **HALF** rest gets two (2) COUNTS (beats)

The **SIXTEENTH** rest gets a quarter (¼) COUNT (beat)

The **QUARTER** rest gets one (1) COUNT (beat)

A rest gets the same value as a note but is counted silently, without playing.

MEASURE   REPEAT SIGN

BAR LINE

The material found in this method will go only to sixteenth notes, although note values continue into thirty-second, sixty-fourth, and one hundred and twenty-eighth notes.

THE SNARE DRUM

STICK POSITIONS

Figure I

Figure II

Figure III

In figure I the hands are placed in the starting position. Try to sit up straight and relax your arms so that they are resting at your sides. Remember that all playing is done with the wrists and **NOT** with the arms.

The right stick should be held between the thumb and index finger, keeping the butt or shaft of the stick in the small of the hand.

The stick in the left hand should rest between the thumb and index finger and be guided by the 4th finger.

Figures II and III show the correct use of a right and left hand beat, all from the starting position. This we will call **ALTERNATE STICKING**. It is advisable to use "alternate sticking" when playing all the exercises in this book, in order to improve coordination of the two hands.

Note: The above information applies to left-handed drummers **IN REVERSE**.

The first exercise of this method deals with whole, half and quarter notes. Start these lines very slowly and **COUNT OUT LOUD**.

WHOLE, HALF AND QUARTER NOTES IN $\frac{4}{4}$ TIME

QUARTER NOTES AND RESTS IN $\frac{4}{4}$ TIME

2.

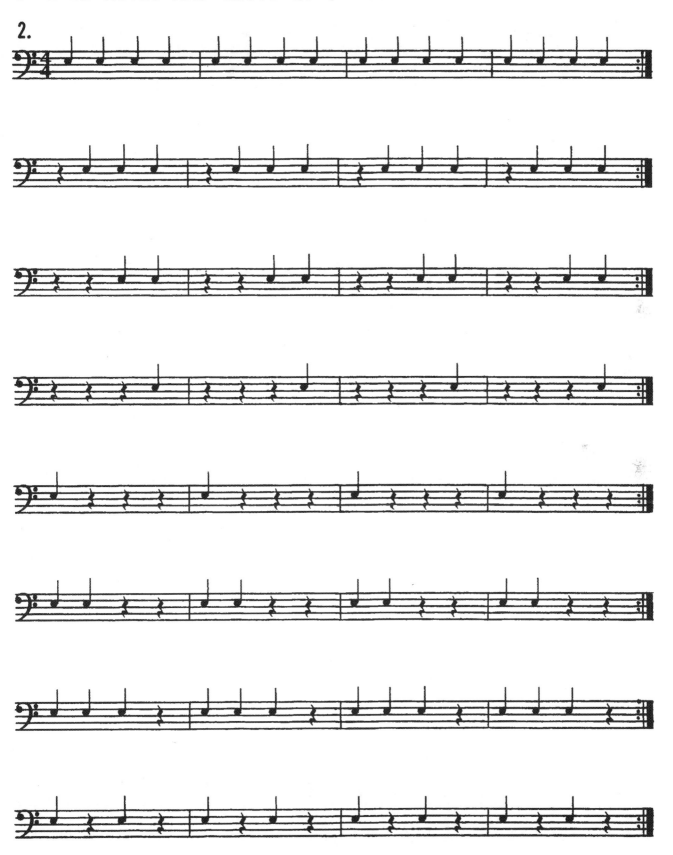

QUARTER NOTES AND RESTS IN $\frac{4}{4}$ TIME (CONTINUED)

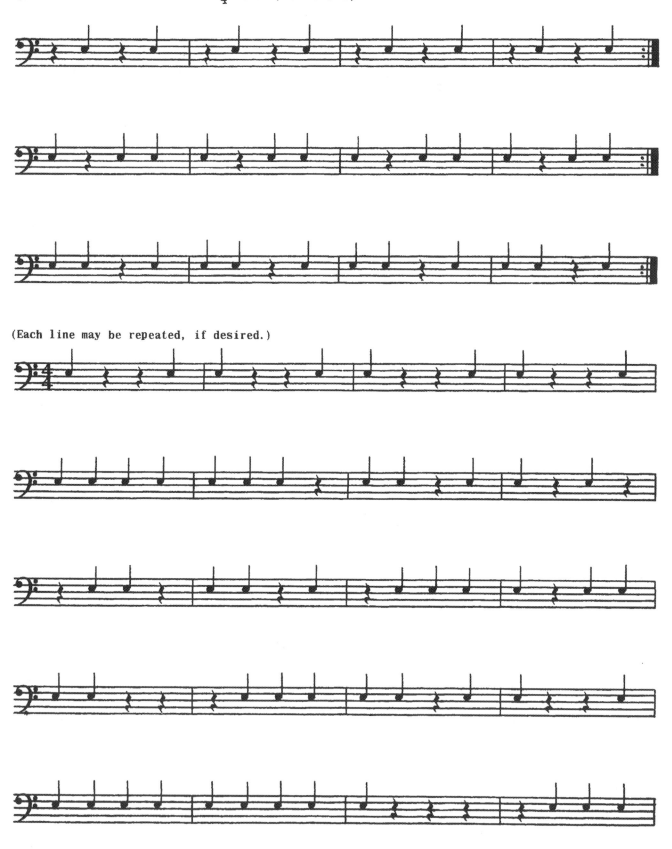

(Each line may be repeated, if desired.)

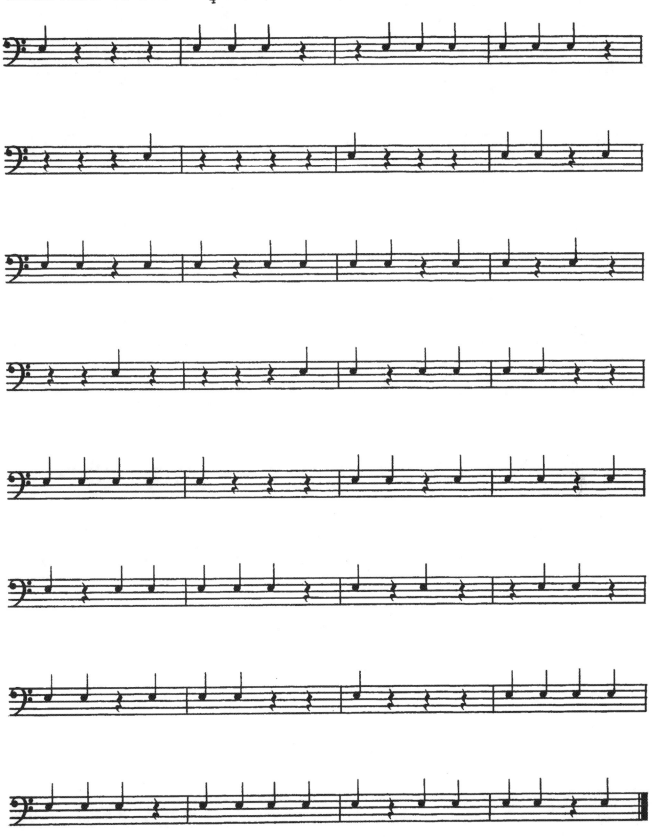

HALF RESTS IN $\frac{4}{4}$ TIME

3. (Each line may be repeated, if desired.)

8

EIGHTH AND QUARTER NOTES IN $\frac{4}{4}$ TIME

(Use Alternate Sticking, RLRL RLRL, etc.)

EIGHTH AND QUARTER NOTES WITH RESTS IN $\frac{4}{4}$ TIME

(Each line may be repeated, if desired)

5.

Remember that an eighth note gets ½ count (beat).

12

SIXTEENTH NOTES IN $\frac{4}{4}$ TIME

There are two ways of playing sixteenth notes. The first way is to use alternate sticking, which is the most common (RLRLRLRL). The second is to use double sticking (RRLLRRLL). This is the preliminary stage for learning the long or double stroke roll.

Remember, a sixteenth note (♪) gets a quarter of a count (beat), so it takes four sixteenth (♫) notes to make a complete count (or beat).

COUNT AS FOLLOWS:

SIXTEENTH AND QUARTER NOTES WITH RESTS IN 4/4 TIME

7.

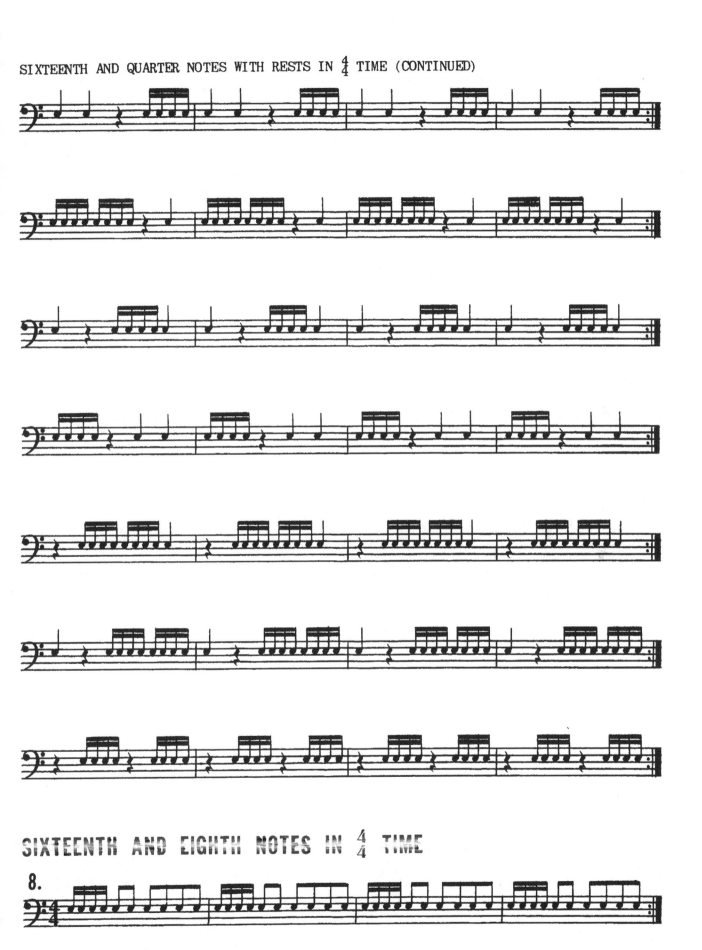

SIXTEENTH AND EIGHTH NOTES IN $\frac{4}{4}$ TIME

8.

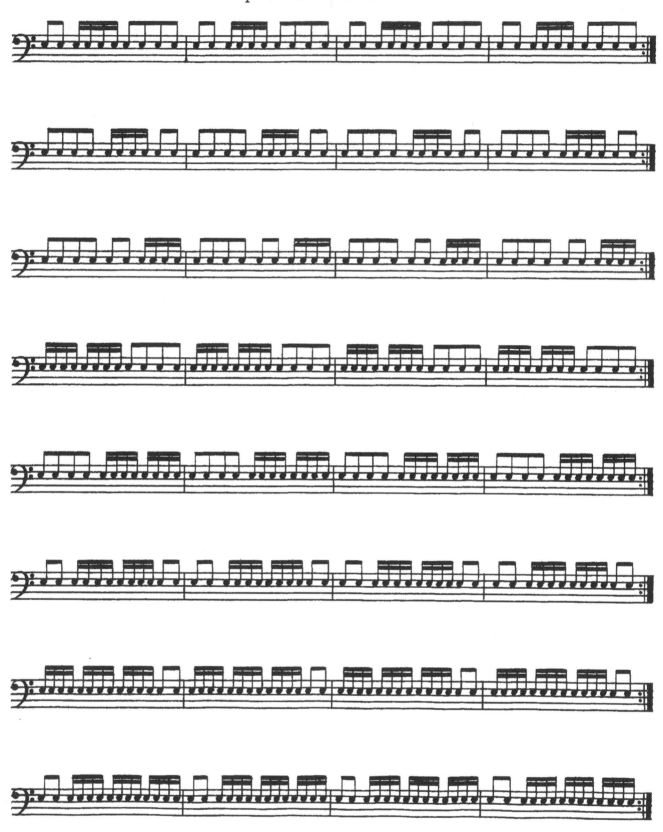

18

SIXTEENTH AND EIGHTH NOTES IN 4/4 TIME (CONTINUED)

SIXTEENTH, EIGHTH AND QUARTER NOTES WITH RESTS IN 4/4 TIME

(Each line may be repeated, if desired.)

9.

SIXTEENTH, EIGHTH AND QUARTER NOTES WITH RESTS IN $\frac{4}{4}$ TIME (CONTINUED)

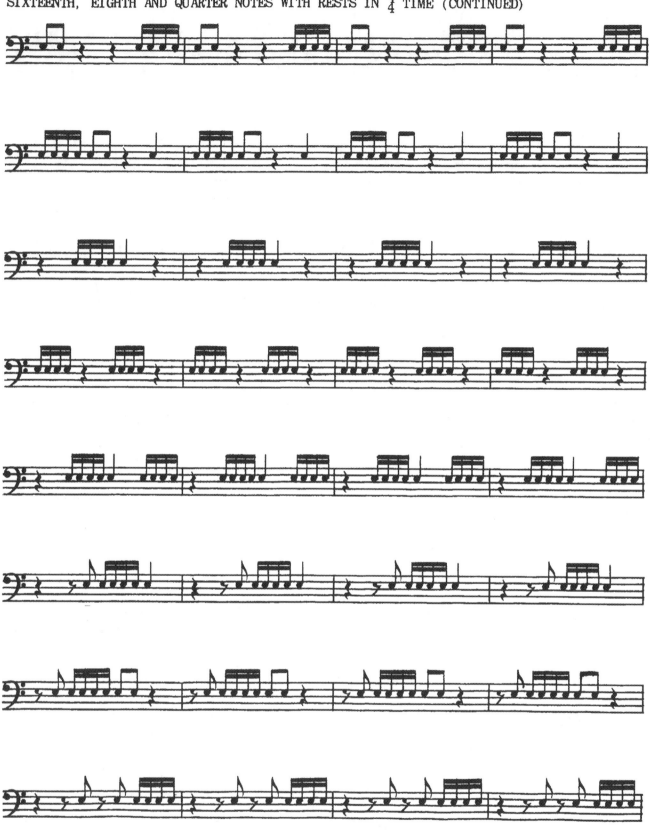

SIXTEENTH, EIGHTH AND QUARTER NOTES WITH RESTS IN $\frac{4}{4}$ TIME (CONTINUED)

$\frac{2}{4}$ TIME

In today's world of music a drummer is expected to play in many different time signatures; even rock music is no longer just 4/4 time. The next exercise will deal with 2/4 time. Most marches, polkas, and heavy latin beats are in 2/4 time. Remember that there are now two counts (beats) per measure.

$\frac{2}{4}$ Two counts (beats) per measure. The quarter note still gets one count (beat).

EXAMPLE: (Notice the time signature.)

1 AN 2 AN

HALF, QUARTER, EIGHTH AND SIXTEENTH NOTES WITH RESTS IN $\frac{2}{4}$ TIME

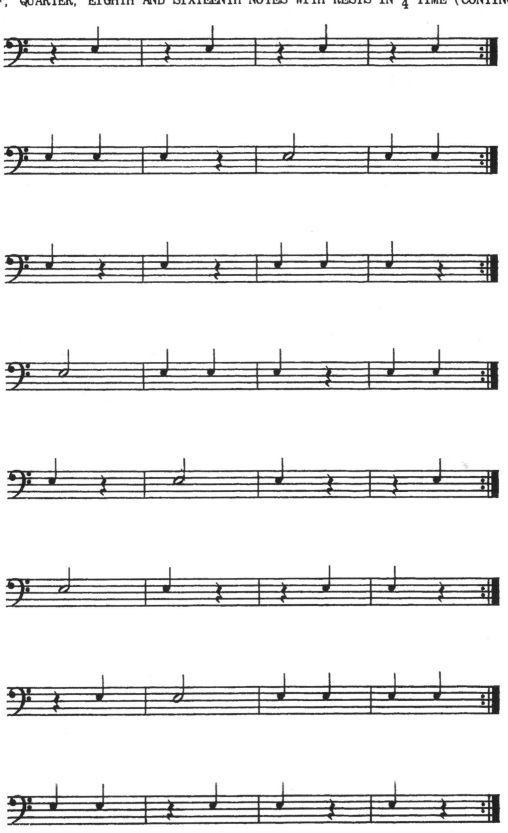

1 & 2 &

1 2 &

24

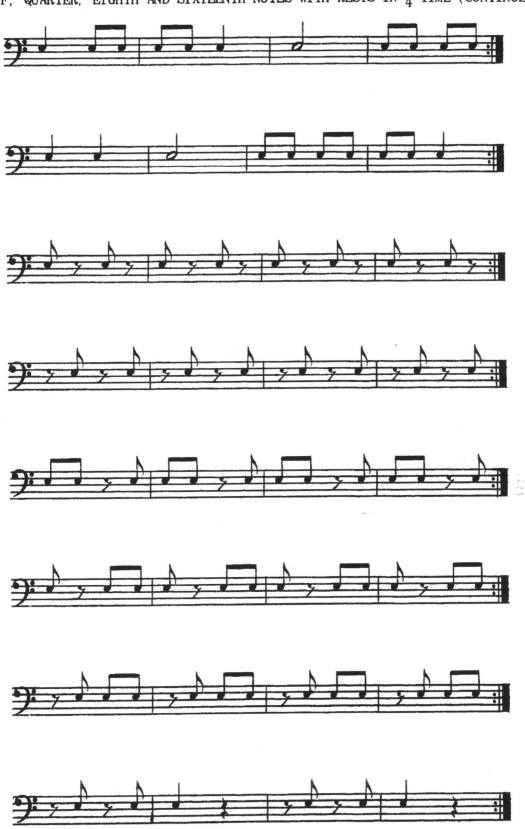

HALF, QUARTER, EIGHTH AND SIXTEENTH NOTES WITH RESTS IN $\frac{2}{4}$ TIME (CONTINUED)

26

27

TRIPLETS

A **triplet** in music, is a group of 3 notes played in the time of two similar notes. They are always indicated by placing the figure 3 opposite the note heads. Example:

In the following exercises, the triplet is a group of three eighth notes combined to sound, feel, and have the same value as a quarter note. When playing triplets one must accent the first beat of each triplet, not to be loud or noticed, but more to be felt. If this accent is not present the triplet tends to sound like straight eighth notes.

When counting triplets try to maintain the feeling of three. Such as; 1-trip-let 2-trip-let 3-trip-let 4-trip-let. When playing triplets fast, count out loud and use the following: 1-ta-ta 2-ta-ta 3-ta-ta 4-ta-ta.

EXAMPLE:

ACCENT to be played harder.

TRIPLETS IN $\frac{4}{4}$ TIME

START SLOWLY AND COUNT OUT LOUD

(Each line may be repeated, if desired.)

TRIPLETS IN $\frac{4}{4}$ TIME (CONTINUED)

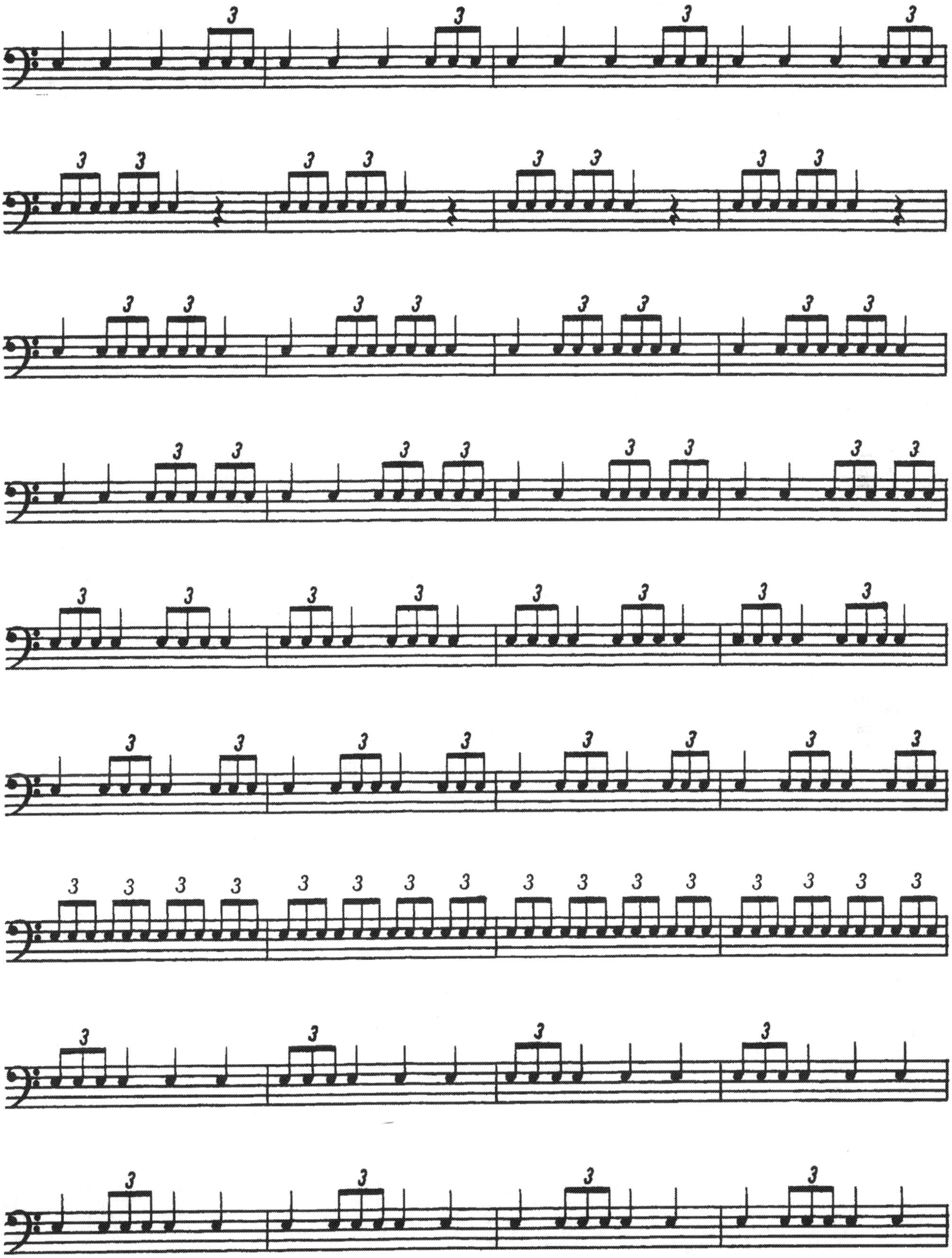

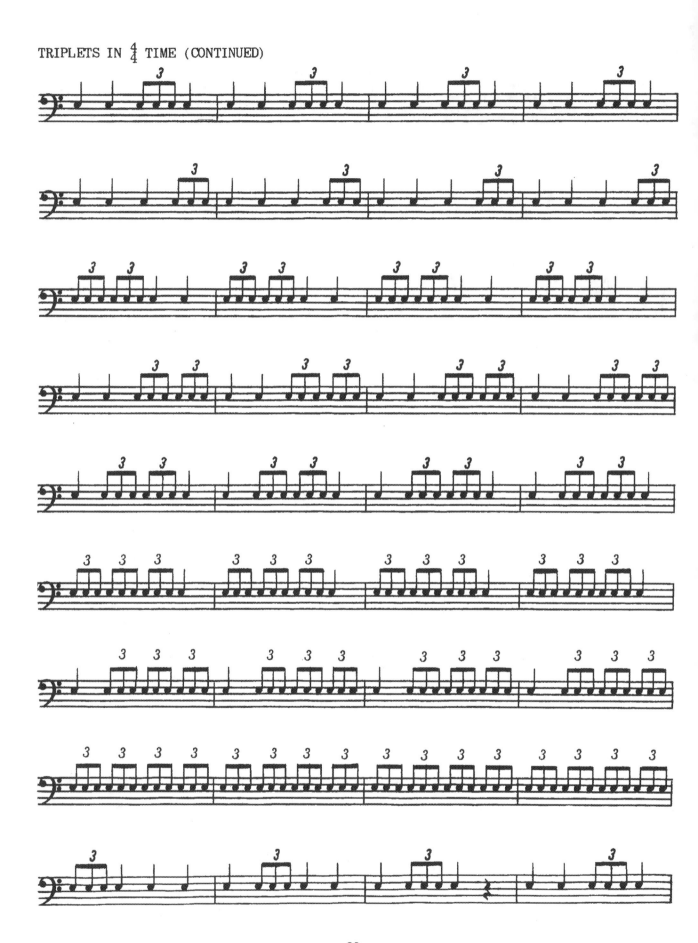

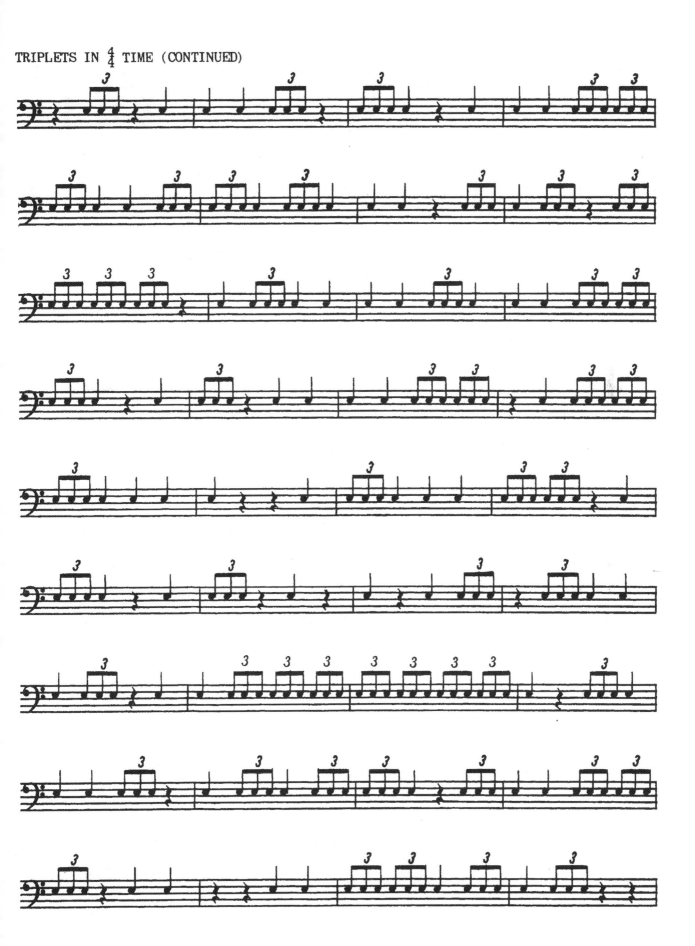

TRIPLETS IN $\frac{4}{4}$ TIME (CONTINUED)

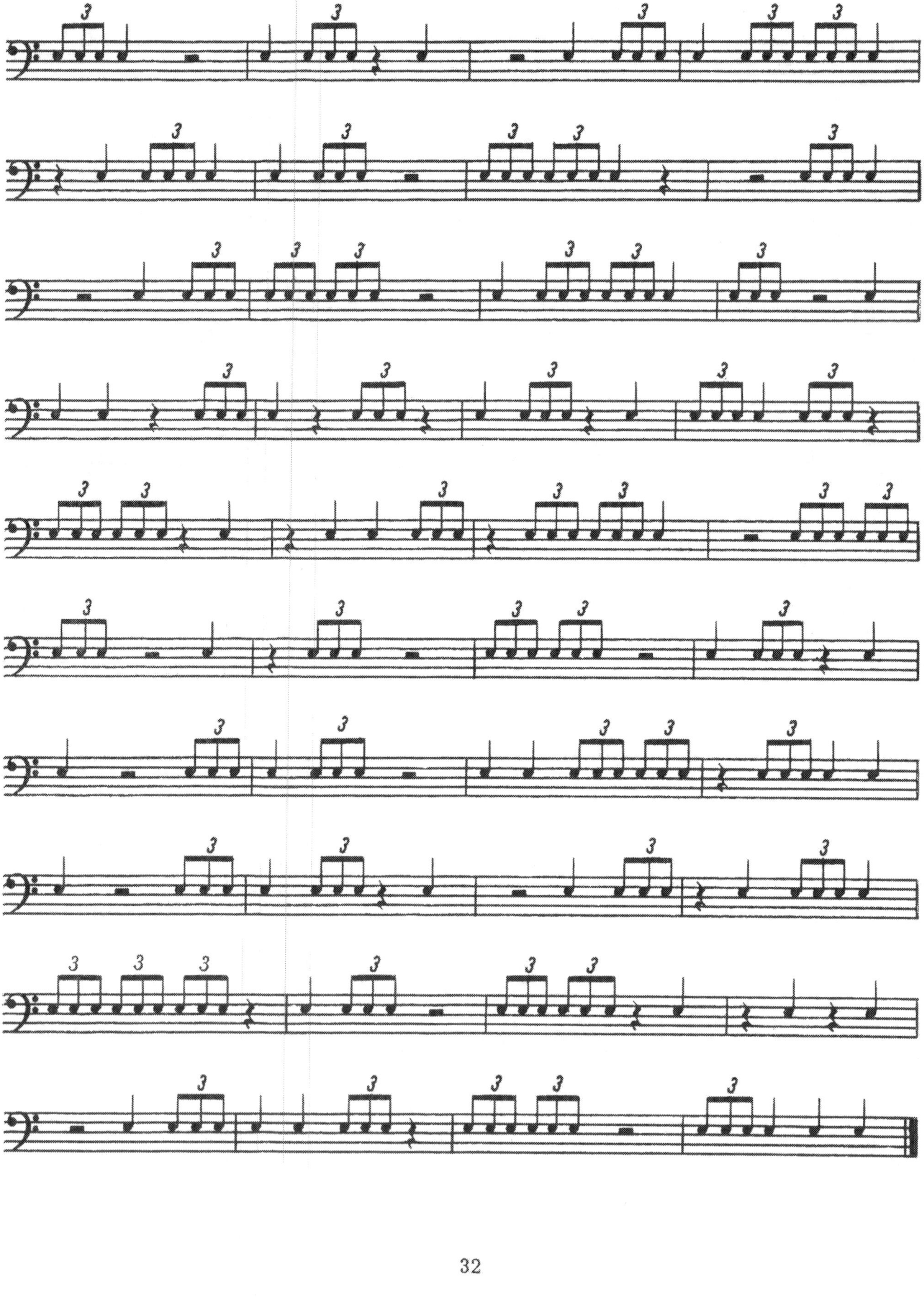

TRIPLETS AND REGULAR EIGHTH NOTES IN $\frac{4}{4}$ TIME

12.

THE BASS DRUM

The bass drum is the most important drum next to the snare drum. It provides a beat or bottom for the band. Years ago the bass drum was used in absence of a string bass. Today the bass drum is used not only to play time but to make accents or kicks for the band. In practicing the next exercises the foot should be flat on the pedal as in figure II. Count out loud and use a metronome whenever possible.

BASS DRUM EXERCISES IN $\frac{4}{4}$ TIME

13. (Each line may be repeated, if desired.)

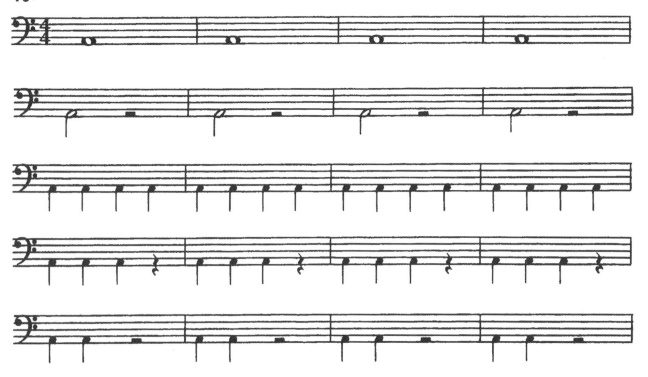

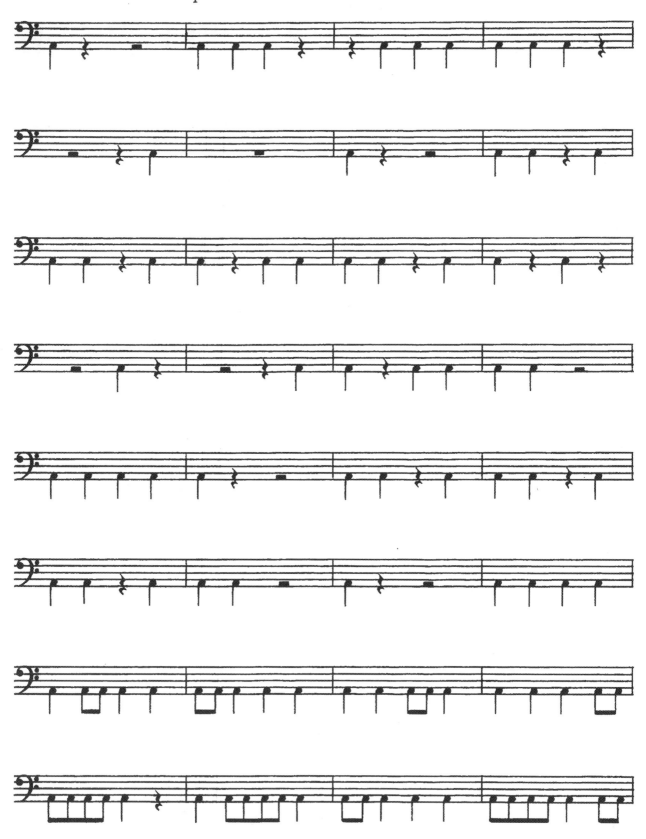

BASS DRUM AND SNARE DRUM EXERCISES IN $\frac{4}{4}$ TIME

14.

BASS DRUM AND SNARE DRUM EXERCISES IN $\frac{4}{4}$ TIME (CONTINUED)

THE HI-HAT OR AFTER-BEAT CYMBALS

The hi-hat cymbals originated in the late twenties when they were mainly used for effects. In the late forties and early fifties they were used for after-beats; now they are used for both.

Today rock drummers use the hi-hat more than any other cymbal to play time. Jazz drummers use the hi-hat not only to play time on after-beats, but also as accents or kicks, which can be played on any beat.

BASS DRUM AND HI-HAT EXERCISES IN $\frac{4}{4}$ TIME

15.   Note: Cymbal notation is usually indicated by a cross note, as:

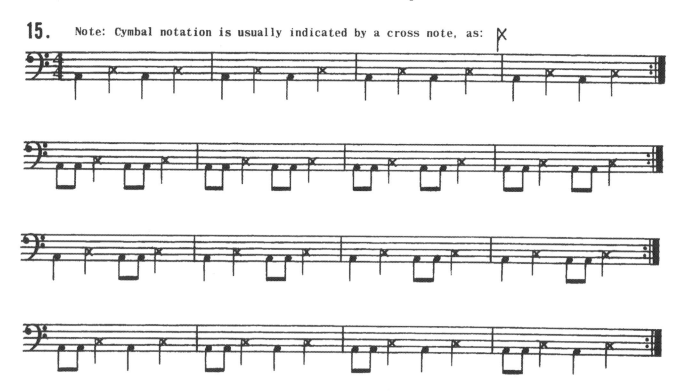

41

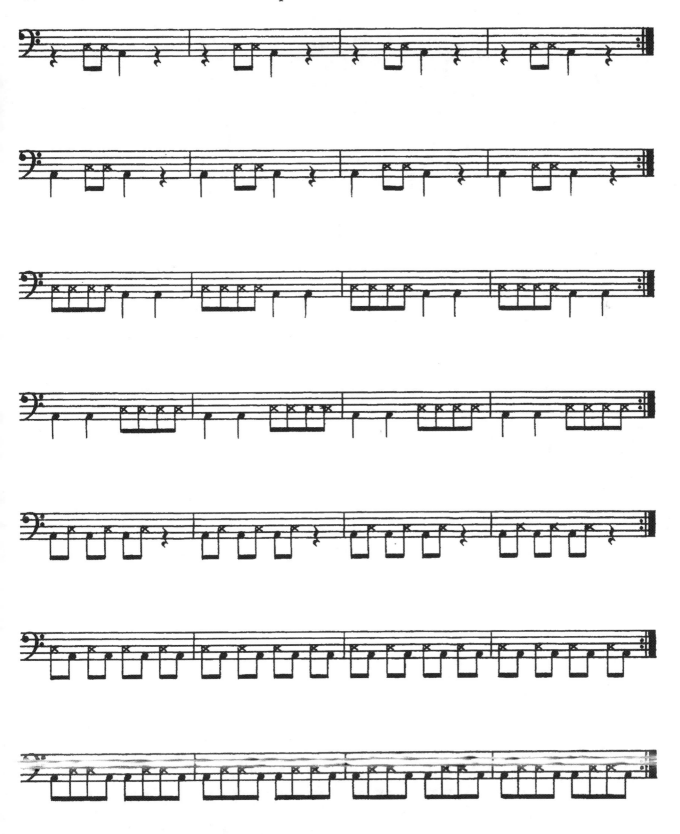

THE RIDE CYMBAL

ROCK

Following is the most common cymbal pattern used for **Rock** drumming:

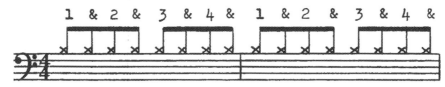

This cymbal pattern is written in eighth notes, and is played on the ride cymbal or the closed hi-hat with the right hand.

JAZZ

Following is the most common cymbal pattern used for **Jazz or Dance** drumming:

Although this pattern is written with dotted-eighth and sixteenth notes (♩. ♪), think in terms of triplets (♪ ♪).

ROCK EXERCISES FOR RIDE CYMBAL WITH SNARE DRUM IN $\frac{4}{4}$ TIME

16.

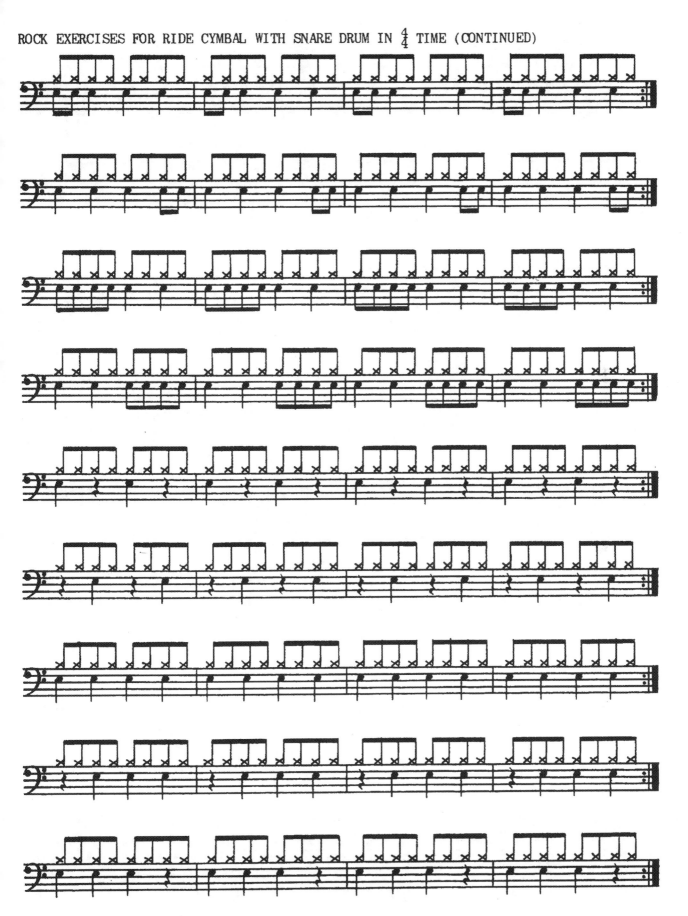

(Each line may be repeated, if desired.)

ROCK EXERCISES FOR RIDE CYMBAL WITH BASS DRUM IN $\frac{4}{4}$ TIME

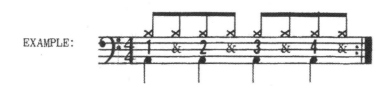

(Each line may be repeated, if desired.)

17.

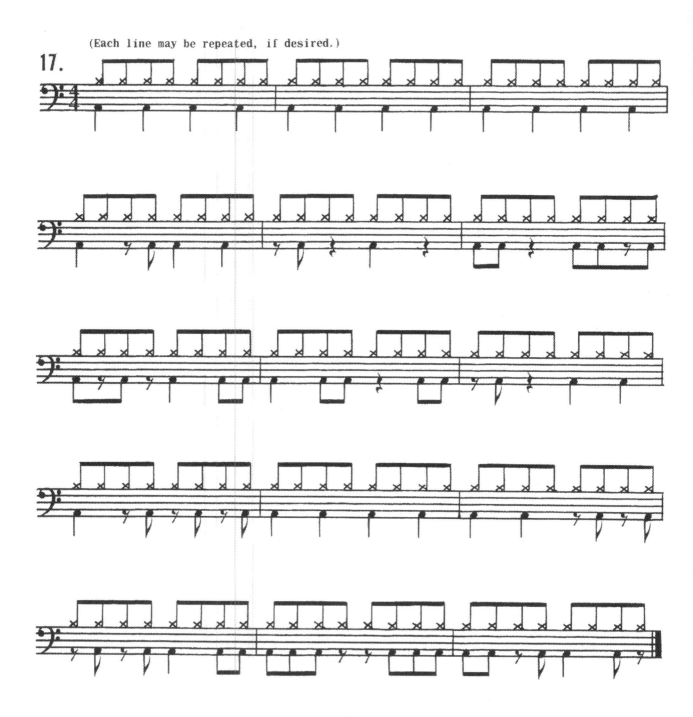

JAZZ EXERCISES FOR RIDE CYMBAL WITH SNARE DRUM IN $\frac{4}{4}$ TIME

18.

JAZZ EXERCISES FOR RIDE CYMBAL WITH SNARE DRUM IN $\frac{4}{4}$ TIME (CONTINUED)

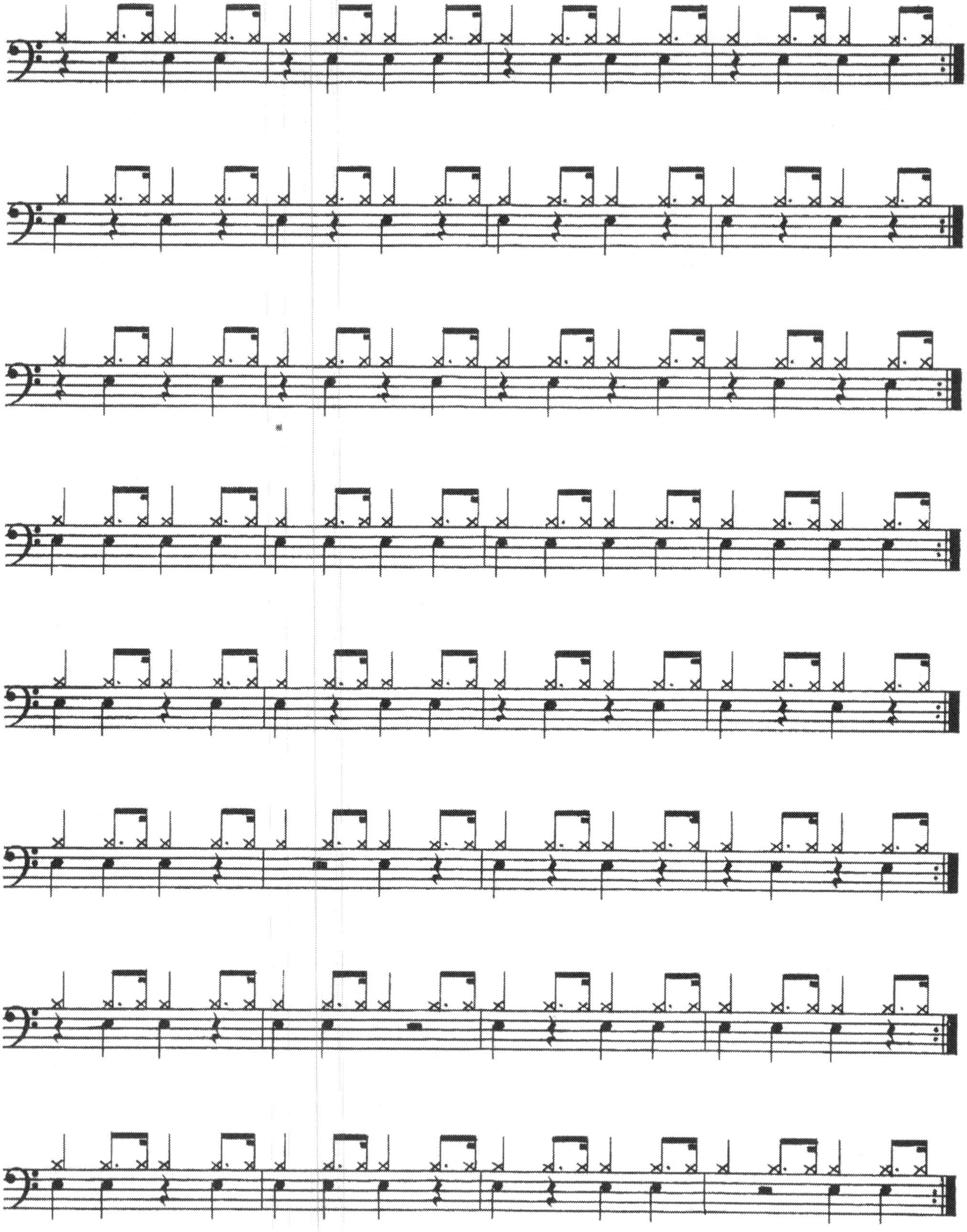

EXERCISES FOR RIDE CYMBAL WITH SNARE DRUM
AND BASS DRUM IN $\frac{4}{4}$ TIME

EXAMPLE:

Right Hand on Ride Cymbal →

Left Hand on Snare Drum →

Right Foot on Bass Drum →

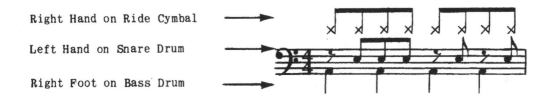

19.

Turn to exercise number 2 and play through exercise number 5, using the right hand on ride cymbal, the left hand on snare drum and the right foot on bass drum. This will insure a stronger feeling of independence when playing rock, jazz or dance music.

COMPLETE INDEPENDENCE

EXAMPLE: (Usually written this way, on one staff.)

Right Hand on Ride Cymbal →

Left Hand on Snare Drum →
Right Foot on Bass Drum →

Left Foot on Hi-hat →

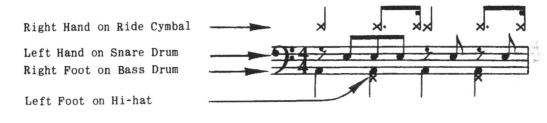

EXAMPLE: (Using Two Staffs)

Right Hand on Ride Cymbal →
Left Hand on Snare Drum →

Left Foot on Hi-hat →
Right Foot on Bass Drum →

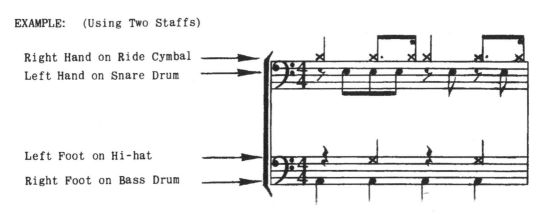

The last set of exercises in this method deals with complete independence of the drum set, including the snare drum, bass drum, ride cymbal and hi-hat.

ROCK EXERCISES FOR COMPLETE DRUM SET IN $\frac{4}{4}$ TIME

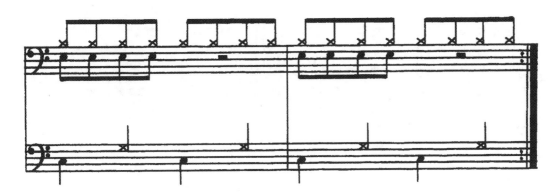

JAZZ EXERCISES FOR COMPLETE DRUM SET IN $\frac{4}{4}$ TIME

Note: Remember to think in terms of triplets and dotted eighths, rather than straight eighths as in previous exercises.

21.

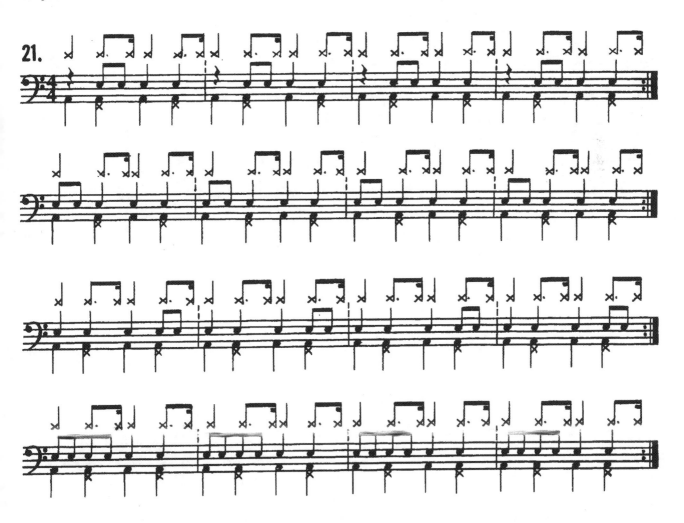

Printed in the United States
By Bookmasters

Drummer Joe Corsello was born and raised in Stamford, Connecticut. He has made a lifetime commitment to playing drums and continually strives to reach new heights in the drumming world.

Joe studied at Berklee College of Music in Boston, Massachusetts under the watchful eye of drum legend Alan Dawson. After leaving Berklee, he enlisted in the U.S. Army and was assigned to the Army Band, stationed in Staten Island, New York.

During his time in the Army, Joe studied with drummer Joe Hunt, who was living in New York City. After completion of his service obligation, Joe went on to tour with the Glenn Miller Orchestra, under the direction of Buddy DeFranco. Joe remained in New York City as house drummer for Michael's Pub, backing jazz artists Red Norvo, Joe Venuti, Dave McKenna, Hank Jones, Zoot Simms and pianist, Marian McPartland.

Some of Joe's latest works can be heard on Big Fish Music's production of cinematic percussion sounds.

Joe's longtime relationship with jazz producer/writer, Michael Cuscuna, brought about the formation of the jazz/rock band, New York Mary, (Arista Records). The band recorded two successful records and toured with the B52's, Patti Smith, Stevie Wonder, and the Tony Williams Lifetime Band.

Joe currently travels with saxophonist, Sonny Rollins, and can be heard on recordings with Rollins, Marian McPartland, Benny Goodman, Steve Marcus, Ralph Lalama, Mike Moore, Sal Salvadore, Gene Bertoncini, Mike Mainieri and numerous others.

U.S. $14.99

ISBN 978-1-4917-9986-4

iUniverse®
www.iuniverse.com

9 781491 799864

51499